THE BOOK OF

TOILET JOKES

Sid Finch

summersdale

THE LITTLE BOOK OF TOILET JOKES

An Hachette UK Company
www.hachette.co.uk

Summersdale Publishers Ltd
Part of Octopus Publishing Group Limited
Carmelite House
50 Victoria Embankment
LONDON
EC4Y 0DZ
UK

www.summersdale.com

Printed and bound in China

ISBN: 978-1-78685-549-7

Substantial discounts on bulk quantities of Summersdale books are available to corporations, professional associations and other organisations. For details contact general enquiries: telephone: +44 (0) 1243 771107 or email: enquiries@summersdale.com.

Contents

Introduction

To help you feel more relaxed during those times of tediousness (and sometimes torture) on the bog – from when your flies are down to when you flush – *The Little Book of Toilet Jokes* is here to provide a little light relief. Packed with a selection of the very best bathroom gags, and divided into chapters for toilet breaks short and long, this little book is guaranteed to have you giggling from the mouth and bubbling from the bum.

And, what's more, once you've done the dreadful deed you can check your poo type by flicking to the descriptive Poo Dictionary at the back of the book.

Say hello to happier times on the lavatory!

One-liners for Quick Toilet Trips

I get diarrhoea
from my parents.

It runs in my jeans.

What happens if
you eat ten cans of
alphabet spaghetti?

You get an enormous
vowel movement.

I was planning to go to the cinema this weekend to watch that new movie, *Constipated* –

but it's not come out yet.

I have watched the prequel, *Diarrhoea*, though.

It leaked and they had to release it early.

What do penguins suffer from when they sit on the toilet for too long?

Polaroids.

What's an ig?

An ice house that doesn't have a toilet.

Two flies are sitting
on a dog poo.
One of them farts.

'Do you mind?!'
says the other one in
disgust. 'Can't you
see I'm eating?'

What did one toilet say
to the other toilet?

'You look flushed.'

**What do you get
if you cross a bear
with a toilet?**

Winnie the Pooh.

**What did Mr Spock
find in the loo?**

The Captain's log.

Did you hear about the constipated mathematician?

He worked it out with a pencil.

Did you hear about the constipated composer?

He had issues with his final movement.

KNOCK KNOCK
'Sir, this is the police, please open this door immediately.'
'Do you mind, I'm having a poo in here.'

'We know, sir, the phone box has glass sides.'

'Hi there, you've reached the incontinence hotline. Please hold...'

For my birthday this year, I was given Sudoku toilet paper. It's useless.

You can only fill it in with number ones and twos.

What do you get when you poo in your overalls?

Dung-arees.

What's brown and sounds like a bell?

Dung.

Today I went to the toilet without my smartphone.

There are 194 tiles on the bathroom wall.

Did you hear the joke about the toilet?

You wouldn't like it, it's too dirty.

Which renowned criminal farted the most?

Jack the Ripper.

**Why couldn't the toilet
paper cross the road?**

It got stuck in a crack!

**Why did the policeman
sit on the toilet?**

To do his duty.

**What did one fly say
to the other fly?**

'Is this stool taken?'

**What's big and brown
and behind the wall?**

Humpty's Dump.

Toilet paper:

what a rip off.

**What's the definition
of a surprise?**

A lumpy fart.

What do toilets and anniversaries have in common?

Men always miss them.

Farting in a lift is wrong...

on so many levels.

If you're an American when you go into the toilet, and an American when you come out, what are you while you're in there?

Eur-o-pean.

What should you do if lightning strikes your lavatory?

Don't panic – it's just a flash in the pan.

How many men
does it take to put
down a toilet seat?

No idea. It's never
happened.

People say laughter
is the best medicine.

Not if you have
diarrhoea, it isn't!

**What do log fires
and wetting yourself
have in common?**

**They both give you
a warm feeling.**

**Did you hear the
one about the toilet
paper that rolled
down the hill?**

**It wanted to get
to the bottom.**

What do you call a superhero in a toilet?

Flush Gordon.

What do you call Clark Kent with the runs?

Poop-erman.

What's the difference between Mozart and a fart?

One is music to your ear; the other is music from your rear.

What do you call someone who refuses to pass wind in public?

A private toot-or.

What is it called when a member of the aristocracy blows off?

A noble gas.

What's the difference between an archaeologist and a flatulist?

One digs for artefacts; the other digs farty acts.

Why couldn't the skeleton break wind in public?

Because he had no guts.

What is the sharpest thing in the world?

A fart; it goes through your pants and doesn't even leave a hole.

Why can't you hear psychiatrists when they use the toilet?

The 'P' is silent.

What do you call a fairy doing a number two?

Stinker Bell.

Did you hear about the man who was distributing leaflets on flatulence awareness?

It was all going well until he let one rip.

Did you hear about the constipated accountant?

He couldn't budget.

**What did the priest
say before he
flushed the toilet?**

Holy c**p!

**Why should you never
fart in church?**

**Because you have
to stay seated in
your pew.**

Why don't boxers need to flush the toilet?

They scare the c**p out of it.

I love my loo.

We've been through a hell of a lot of s**t together.

What do you get if you scoff down a big plate of onions and baked beans?

Tear gas.

What did the sanitary towel say to the fart?

'You are the wind beneath my wings.'

Jokes for Solid Sessions on the Bog

Two novice nuns are preparing to be initiated into their order. Their Mother Superior tells them to go and commit one sin to get rid of any urges to perform unholy acts in the future.

They return the next day, the first nun looking very upset and the second smiling slyly.

'Well, Sisters, what did you do?' asks their Mother Superior.

'I acted in anger and shouted at an elderly lady on the bus,' says the first. 'I felt so bad I spent all night crying into my pillow.'

At this, the second nun's smile bursts into full-blown laughter.

'And, Sister, what did you do? Why are you laughing?' asks the senior nun.

'Oh, I farted on her pillow!'

A woman goes to see her GP
with a flatulence issue.

'How can I help?' asks the doctor.

'Well, to be blunt, I just can't stop farting,'
replies the woman. 'But it's not really an
issue because the strange thing is they don't
smell or make any noise. I mean, I've done
several in the past minute while I've been
sitting here but you won't have noticed.'

'Right,' says the doctor. 'First of all,
here's some decongestant to start
unblocking your nose. Come back next
week and I'll book you a hearing test.'

A young girl is wandering down a country lane when she sees a local farmer with a huge truck-full of cow manure.

The girl asks him what he's going to do with all the cow poo.

'Oh, I'm taking it home to put on my strawberries,' says the farmer.

'Yuk!' replies the girl. 'Mum normally puts cream and sugar on ours.'

A guy has been dating a woman for over a year. Thinking she could be 'the one' and being something of a traditionalist, he goes to the woman's father to ask his permission for her hand in marriage.

The father is not amused. Knowing the suitor is in a lowly paid job he says, rudely, 'With the money you have, you wouldn't even be able to pay for my daughter's toilet paper.'

'Don't worry,' he fires back. 'I won't bother asking her if she's full of c**p.'

Pedro is having a party at his house for New Year's Eve. Most of the guests pace themselves but best friend Sergio is downing shot after shot. Eventually Sergio stumbles off in the direction of the toilet. A short while afterwards, the rest of the party-goers hear Sergio making very loud noises. At first everyone ignores it, but when it continues, Pedro feels he'd better investigate.

'What's all the screaming about in here?' shouts Pedro from outside the closed door. 'This is supposed to be a nice party.'

'I'm just sitting here on the toilet,' rants Sergio, 'and every time I try to flush, something comes up and grabs my b***s.'

So, Pedro pushes the door open to see what's happening. 'You idiot!' he shouts. 'You're sitting on the mop bucket!'

Bob: 'I didn't fart in front of my wife until after we were married.'

Bill: 'Oh, really, that's commendable.'

Bob: 'Yeah, it was a huge relief for me, but I don't think the wedding party was impressed.'

Chuck, Randy and Dustin find a novelty pub on their night out which has a musical toilet. The toilet sings a song to whoever sits on it.

Chuck goes in first. When he comes out, the other two ask him, 'So, what did it sing for you?'

Chuck replies, 'It sang "Blue Suede Shoes".'

Next up, it's Randy. When he emerges, Chuck and Dustin are eager to know the tune.

'It sang "Hey, Jude" for me,' he replies.

Finally, it's Dustin's turn. Unlike the other two, when he comes back out he's looking pretty sheepish. 'What happened?' ask the others. 'What song did it sing?'

'Er, "Do You See What I See?"'

A girl in school is getting desperate for the toilet but is too embarrassed to put her hand up to ask the teacher in case the other children laugh at her.

Eventually she can take no more and calls out, 'Can I go to the bathroom, please Miss?'

'OK, Rosa,' the teacher replies, 'but first I'd like you to say the alphabet for the class.'

'A-B-C-D-E-F-G-H-I-J-K-L-M-N-O-Q-R-S-T-U-V-W-X-Y-Z!' she shouts in a hurry.

'Hang on,' says the teacher. 'Where's the "P"?'

'Er... halfway down my leg.'

A teacher is getting her class of young children to use adverbs appropriately in a sentence.

She asks Timmy to think of a sentence using the word 'definitely'.

'Miss, do farts have lumps in them?' he replies.

'What?!' replies Miss, exasperated. 'Of course not, Timmy.'

'Oh, then I have definitely pooed my pants... '

An old drunk staggers out of the
pub at closing time, rests against
a parked car and starts having a
pee, in full view of a policeman.

The officer walks over to have a word.
'Excuse me, sir, you cannot do that. It's a
£15 on-the-spot fine for urinating in public.'

'Fair enough,' slurs the old guy,
and hands him a £20 note.

'Thanks, but I haven't got any
change,' says the policeman.

'No bother,' says the bloke with a
wink. 'You keep it 'cos I let rip a
couple of farts just now too.'

A sport-loving couple are sitting in bed before lights out. Suddenly, the man farts and shouts, 'Five points!'

'What!?' says his wife, who's appalled and confused.

'It's fart rugby.'

A couple of minutes later she gets in on the act. 'That's a try, we're even,' she says.

Straight away, he does another to retake the lead: Ten–five.

His wife then lets go of a spectacular one. 'Woah! That's a try and a conversion,' she boasts. 'Ten–twelve!'

Not to be outdone at his own game, the man spends the next few minutes trying to let a massive one go… but he poos the bed instead.

'Yuk, what's that?' asks his wife.

'Half-time,' he says sheepishly. 'Swap sides.'

A man is sitting in a crowded dentists' waiting room. Out of nowhere, he gets the urge to do a big fart. He does his best to hold it in but, after a couple of minutes, he lets it go. It turns out to be rather loud, so he starts acting nonchalantly, hoping no one's noticed. At first he pretends to look at his phone, and then leans over to the woman next to him and asks, 'Could you pass me today's newspaper, please?'

'No,' she says, 'but if you reach out of the window you should be able to grab some leaves off that bush.'

Blackbeard the pirate always puts on a red shirt whenever it looks like a skirmish with a rival crew is about to start.

One day, while patrolling the deck, his cabin boy asks him the reason for this ritual.

'It's just in case I get shot,' he explains. 'I don't want the crew to see the blood on me and worry.'

Just at that moment, a particularly bloodthirsty crew boards the ship and slowly starts towards him with their sabres raised.

Blackbeard starts nudging the cabin boy rather urgently. 'Er... can you fetch me my brown trousers, please?'

A man goes into a public toilet for a poo. He's just sat down when he hears a voice from the next cubicle say, 'Hello, how are you?'

He's embarrassed but thinks he'd better reply out of courtesy. 'I'm fine, thanks.'

Then the voice asks, 'So what are you up to?'

'Well, just doing the same as you, sitting here, obviously.'

Then the voice asks, 'Can I come over?'

This is getting ridiculous, thinks the man. 'Actually, I'm a little busy right now.'

The voice then says, 'Hang on, I'm going to have to call you back, there's some weirdo next door who keeps answering all my questions.'

A little old man goes to see the doctor
to discuss a problem 'down below'.
As he's hard of hearing, he takes along
his wife in case he needs her to interpret
anything he doesn't understand.

After examining the man, the doctor
says, 'Well, I'm not sure, but at this stage
I think we'd better get a stool sample,
a urine sample and a sperm sample.'

The old man looks at his wife and
shouts, 'What did he say?'

'He says he wants your pants.'

A landlady is standing behind the bar when the door of her pub swings open and in trots a pig. 'Pint, please?' the pig asks.

'Er... certainly,' says the shocked woman.

The pig downs it in one and then asks where the gents' is.

'Oh, down there, on the left,' replies the woman.

Suddenly, another pig comes in. He orders two pints, downs them and also asks to use the loo.

The landlady is still shaking her head in wonder at all this when a third pig comes in. He orders three pints, downs them and... just sits there.

'Aren't you going to ask where the toilet is?' says the landlady.

'No,' replies the pig, 'I'm going wee wee wee all the way home.'

A dad is watching TV when his three-year-old daughter comes in. She's holding a little cup and saucer and she wants to play tea parties. Ah, how cute, he thinks. It's only water, of course, but he joins in.

'Mmm, delicious,' he says, taking a sip.

Just then, his wife comes in and shoots him a look. 'Brian, you do know the only place she can reach water is from the toilet bowl, right?'

It's Valentine's Day and a wife
sends her husband a romantic text
message to mark the occasion.

'I want you, I desire you,
wherever you are and whatever
you are doing, think of me,
your one true love.'

Her husband texts back:
'I'm in the toilet at the
moment, Sandra, I'm going
to have to get back to you.'

A couple and their friend Fatima are out having lunch. 'My house is packed full of great tech,' says Harry to Fatima. 'Take my bathroom, for instance. When I get up in the night to go to the loo, the light turns on by itself!'

His wife, Joan, looks ashen-faced at this news but keeps quiet.

A few minutes later, Harry gets up to go to the toilet. With him out of earshot, Fatima asks, 'Are you OK, Joan? You looked troubled.'

'Yes, sorry,' she replies. 'I just realised why the fridge has been getting so filthy!'

Tim is at his grandparents' house for Sunday lunch. After feasting on cauliflower cheese, broccoli and lamb, he knows he has to let one go. He slyly lifts a buttock off the seat and tries to let one out quietly, but fails – the parp is not overly loud, but certainly audible.

Straight away, Tim's granddad looks at the family dog, sitting at Tim's feet, and shouts, 'Bailey!'

Delighted, but still feeling uncomfortable, Tim lets out another fart, this time louder.

Again, his granddad yells at the dog.

With growing confidence, Tim lets out a real honker.

'Bailey!' shouts Tim's granddad again. 'Get away from that dirty child before he s**ts on you!'

A single young man who hasn't long left the family home is at the supermarket, stocking up on items for his new rented flat.

He comes across some ultra-cheap toilet brushes – buy one get one free. 'Brilliant! What a great idea,' he thinks to himself and buys half a dozen.

Within a fortnight, however, he goes back to using toilet paper.

A girl comes home from school one day and proudly tells her parents that she answered a question correctly in class.

Happy for their daughter's achievement, they ask, 'And what was the question?'

Smiling, the girl replies, 'Who farted?'

A man travelling on a train really needs a poo after having a dodgy takeaway the night before.

He locks himself in the cubicle and sits down. Relief. But just as he's in the middle of going, there's an impatient knock on the toilet door.

'Ticket, please?' shouts the inspector.

'Hang on, not right now,' the man yells back, 'I'm having a s**t!'

'I don't believe you, can you pass it under the door?'

'No problem,' says the man, sliding it under. 'I think the lumpy bits are egg fried rice.'

A bad man dies and goes to hell.

The devil meets him at the gates. 'OK, Steve, you get a choice. You can pick either one of two torture rooms in which to spend eternity.'

Oh well, every cloud... he thinks.

The first room contains millions of people being force-fed chilli sauce whilst being repeatedly poked in the eyes with sharp sticks.

The second room is full of people standing up to their shoulders in vomit, drinking champagne.

'This doesn't look so bad,' says Steve. 'I'll take this room.' So, the devil sends him in to spend the rest of his days. Just as he gets settled into the vomit, champagne flute in hand, an announcement comes over the speakers.

'Right. Break time's over. Back to your handstands!'

Carol gets really annoyed when her husband doesn't use air freshener or even open the window after doing a poo. One morning, over coffee, she sees an advert on the internet that could solve her problem.

'This is what we need, Pierre,' she says. 'An odourless loo.'

Pierre shrugs. It's five times the price of a normal one, owing to its special feature, but when his back is turned, she orders one and it arrives two days later.

A specialist plumber from the toilet manufacturer soon arrives to fit it and even takes the old toilet away.

'There,' says Carol to her disgruntled husband, 'I can breathe easy now.'

The following morning, Carol goes into the bathroom after her husband to smell the results. It stinks. And for once Pierre has even opened the window!

Distraught, she's straight on the phone to the plumber.

'This odourless toilet is useless,' she rages. 'You'd better get round here now.'

The plumber can't understand it. He's installed dozens in the past, all without complaint.

He arrives at the house a couple of hours later and heads up to the bathroom.

'Well, no wonder it stinks,' he exclaims, 'you've left a s**t in it!'

A dog walks into a bar
and jumps up on a stool in
front of the bartender.

'Hi, there, what's it to be?'
asks the bartender.

'Well, man, it's my birthday
today,' says the dog.
'How about a free drink?'

The bartender turns, looks at
the dog and nods his head,
'Sure, pal, toilet's right
down the corridor.'

Two five-year-old boys are standing at the toilet to pee. One says, 'Your thingy doesn't have any skin on it!'

'Yeah, I've been circumcised,' the other replies.

'What does that mean?'

'It means they cut the skin off the end.'

'Jeez. How old were you when that happened?'

'My mum said I was two days old.'

'Wow. Did it hurt?' the first kid asks inquiringly.

'You bet it hurt. I didn't walk for over a year!'

A husband and wife are chatting about their strengths and weaknesses.

'I really admire you, Karen. You're so calm. I know I can be hard to live with. And when I get angry and start shouting sometimes, you never rise to the bait. I wish I could be so placid like you. I don't know how you do it.'

'It's simple, really,' she says. 'I clean the inside of the toilet.'

'Hey!? How does that help?' he asks.

'Oh, I use your toothbrush, darling!'

A newly married couple have invited some friends round for a dinner party. They've had pork belly, dauphinoise potatoes and sprouts for their main course and by the time they get to the cheese course, the sprouts are starting to repeat on Oleg, the male host.

He's getting stomach cramps and pretty soon his pains give way to a powerful and extremely loud fart. He's mortified when the table suddenly falls silent and, eager to deflect the blame and avoid embarrassment with his new wife, he shoots a look to one of his friends.

'Oh, Sergei, stop that immediately please.'

'Certainly, Oleg,' he replies. 'Let me know which way it was heading.'

A posh couple are travelling to London on the train; first class, of course. After a while, a visibly inebriated man bursts into the carriage and sits near them. Everyone tuts but no one tells him he needs to move. After mumbling incoherently to himself for five minutes, the drunk suddenly leaps to his feet and shouts: 'MAY I HAVE YOUR ATTENTION, PLEASE?' and lets out a tremendous fart.

The posh man's wife is extremely embarrassed and has to leave the carriage momentarily to gather herself. Her husband is quite appalled and feels he must say something.

'Excuse me,' he says, 'do you realise you just broke wind before my wife?'

'Oh, I'm sorry,' says the drunk. 'I didn't know it was her turn.'

A man walks into a large supermarket to do the weekly shop. He's unfamiliar with the layout of the shop, and it takes him ages to find anything. After searching in vain for toiletries for the best part of half an hour, he flags down one of the sales assistants to help him. 'Where can I find the toilet paper, please?' he asks.

'I think it's aisle six. What colour are you after?' she replies.

'Oh, white is fine. I'll do the colouring myself.'

A pirate is sitting in a bar. He has
a wooden leg, a hook for one hand
and a patch over one eye.

Another man starts a conversation with him.
'I'm curious, how did you lose your leg?'

'Arrrgh!' says the pirate, 'I got keelhauled
for treason. Me leg was hanging
off by the end so it had to go.'

'That's awful!' says the man. 'And
you've only got one hand, too... ?'

'That's right,' says the pirate, 'I had
gangrene in it after I came off worse in a
sword fight. The captain cut it off for me.'

'Wow, that's terrible,' the man says.
'So, how did you lose your eye?'

'A seagull s**t in it!'

'A seagull!' says the man, surprised. 'I didn't
know seagull poo was that dangerous?'

'Well it isn't really, but it was me first
day with the hook, you see...'

Lying in the marital bed one night, a man shifts uneasily between the sheets. He needs to let one go but he's trying to do it subtly.

In the end he releases a silent one and then lifts the quilt to air it out.

'Blimey, that stinks!' shouts his wife.

It must have been bad, thinks the man. She's downstairs making a cup of tea.

A man walks into a jewellery shop, looking to buy a watch. A particularly large and ornate gold one catches his eye. As he bends down to get a closer look, he accidentally breaks wind. A shop assistant goes up to him and asks if she can be of any help.

'Yes,' replies the man. 'As a matter of fact, I'm interested in this watch. How much is it?'

'With respect, sir, if you farted just looking at it, you'll s**t yourself when you hear the price.'

Two school-age brothers are sitting on
the sofa watching TV. The youngest
one suddenly catches an awful smell
in his nostrils and grimaces.

'Yuk! Have you farted?' he asks his brother.

'Me?! No!' says the older one.

'You must have. That stinks.
I bet you a fiver you have.'

'You're on,' says the older one, smugly.
And with that he pulls down his pants and
shows him the contents. 'There. I told
you it wasn't a fart. Cough up, please!'

One day Amir walks past his colleague Tim and is met with a full-on view of him pooing.

'Come on, Tim, that's disgusting,' he says.

'But I really like doing it with the door wide open,' explains Tim.

'I get that. But you shouldn't be going in the car at all!'

An elderly couple are at their local cinema for the matinee, as they are every Sunday.

Midway through the film, the husband starts shifting uncomfortably in his seat. He's trying to figure out the best way to let out a discreet fart.

Shortly afterwards, he leans over and whispers to his wife, 'Don't tell anyone, but I just blew off. It was silent though. What should I do?'

'Well you should put a new battery in your hearing aid for a start,' she replies.

The Poo Dictionary: What's Yours?

Bad Hangover Poo

This one always follows a 'session'. The poo is a nasty consistency and it smells really bad. The whole experience is made worse by your crippling hangover.

Bunch of Grapes

A wonderful collection of small turds, bound together in a cluster.

Bunny Poo

When you fire out a succession of little round ones – like a bag of small chocolates – which make tiny splashing sounds as they hit the water.

The Steam Engine

You sit there all cramped up and fart a lot, but no s**t is forthcoming. This one is sometimes called a 'political s**t', since there's a lot of hot air but no end product.

Five-Second Warning

This baby is coming out whether you like it or not, so you'd better be within touching distance of a lav. It will be showing through before you've got your trousers down.

Pale and Pasty

A poo with a ghoulish pallor – all pale yellowy-white. Time to think about improving your diet.

The Poltergeist

You know you've done
a s**t; there's evidence
on the toilet paper, but
the log is nowhere to
be seen in the bowl.

Porridge Poo

The type of s**t that comes
out like lumpy toothpaste
with seemingly no
end in sight.

Posh Poop

This poo has no odour and is exclusive to royalty.

Liquid Explosion

A yellow-brown liquid shoots out of your bum and splashes all over the toilet bowl. Not for the squeamish.

Ring of Fire

This one occurs after you've eaten hot, spicy food. Your tongue burns while you're eating it and your a**e follows suit the next morning.

Splash Attack

This s**t catapults into the bowl, sideways and at speed, causing an upward explosion of water that leaves you feeling rather soggy around the cheeks.

The Aftershock

This s**t is so offensive to the human nose and throat that some say it has a half-life. Certainly, the toilet should be a no-go zone for at least eight hours afterwards.

The Anaconda

This poo is fairly soft, about as thick as your thumb, and at least 1 metre long.

The Behemoth

This s**t fills the entire bowl and simply will NOT flush unless broken into smaller chunks. A wire coat hanger works well. This kind of poo usually occurs while you're at the home of an elderly relative.

The Brick

Hurts like childbirth and leaves you wishing you'd had an epidural before attempting it.

The Buoy

Even after the fourth flush it's still floating in the bowl.

The Crash-Diet S**t

You cp so much, you leave the toilet several kilograms lighter than when you went in.**

The Dangler

This one clings to your bum for dear life, refusing to drop. A bit of bouncing and shaking is usually required to cut it loose.

The Emergency Plumber

This monstrous s**t blocks up the toilet, possibly causing water to overflow.

The Groaner

So large it feels
like it's coming out
sideways. Can only be
helped on its way
with some serious
moaning and
groaning.

The Farmer

A poo that inexplicably contains sweetcorn, even though you last ate sweetcorn six months ago.

The Peek-a-Poo

Now you see it, now you don't – it keeps popping in and out. Requires patience and muscle control.

The Pick-Me-Up

This poo occurs after a lengthy period of constipation. Ahhh. Feel the release of those endorphins.

The Record Breaker

A poo so remarkable that
it should be recorded
for future generations.
Remember to collect
photographic evidence.

The Ritual

An orderly, leisurely
movement that occurs at
the same time each day
and is accomplished by
reading a newspaper.

The Rollercoaster

This one's such a beast to get out and requires so much shouting, screaming, bouncing and wriggling in order to do so, it's like you're at the fairground.

The S**t-Off-a-Shovel

It comes out so slick, clean and easy that you don't even feel it. There's no trace on the paper. You have to peer in the toilet to make sure you actually did one.

The Snake Charmer

This very long, thin s**t is so named because it coils itself like icing on a cupcake at the bottom of the bowl. Poke it with a stick to subdue it.

The Sticky Icky

This poo has the consistency of treacle – however many times you wipe your a**e it just doesn't get clean.

The Surprise Package

This is the sort of package you really don't want; a poo that arrives out of the blue at an inopportune time.

The Toxic Dump

A s**t that emits a truly rancid, lung-burning smell. Just flush quick and get out of there before you pass out.

Twins

You're all done wiping, and you're about to stand up when you realise... there's another one waiting to come out.

If you're interested in finding out more about our books, find us on Facebook at **Summersdale Publishers** and follow us on Twitter at **@Summersdale**.

www.summersdale.com